Al-Khwarizmi

The Great Mathematician

Author

Rafia Rehman

Illustrator

Muhammad Yousaf Rana

Additional Contributors

Dr. Abdul Rehman
Umair Zia

In Collaboration with

Habib ur Rehman Research Foundation

And

Integrity-Humbleness-Compassion

Knowledge is the seal of the kingdom of Suleiman: The whole world is form, knowledge is its spirit

Because of this virtue, the creatures of the seas, and those of mountain and plain are helpless before mankind

Maulana Jalal'u'Din Rumi

163 A.H. (780 A.D.) to 235 A.H. (850 A.D.)

The illustrations of Al-Khwarizmi in this book are based on the artist's imagination on how he may have looked like.

On a cold January day, the six friends had gathered at Ezzah's house to work on their math homework. They could see heavy snow falling through the window. Everything outside was starting to get covered with a beautiful white blanket of snow. Ezzah's dad had turned on the fireplace. The crackling sound of burning wood and its yellow glow made the environment warm and cozy.

Heba was helping Saya and Kabens, who were struggling to grasp the concept of fractions. A little frustrated, Kabens exclaimed, "who came up with these concepts?"

"When will we ever get to use them?", added, Saya.

Just then Ezzah's Mommy brought the pizza that she had baked for the kids. The aroma of the freshly baked dough and bubbling cheese brought a smile on everyone's face. As Mommy started to slice up the pizza, Heba thought of an idea to use the pizza to teach fractions to Saya and Kabens.

"We are starting off with one big round pizza," Heba said, and then questioned Saya and Kabens, "how many slices do we need so each of us gets one slice?"

"Six," said Kabens, "there are six of us so we need to cut the Pizza in six equal slices. That way each of us will get one slice."

"Excellent," remarked Heba and continued, "will each of us get to eat the whole pizza?"

"No," answered Saya.

"Will we each get to eat one-half of the Pizza?" Heba asked another question.

"No," answered both Saya and Kabens in unison.

"Then how much do you think each of us will get to eat?"

"We will cut the pizza in six parts. Which means that each of us will get to eat one part of six or one-sixth (1/6) of the Pizza," said Saya.

"That's right," added Kabens.

With a smile, Heba remarked, "both of you have just solved a real problem of fractions. Fractions are used to describe equal parts of a whole object. In this case, one pizza is going to be divided up into six equal parts. Each of us will get to enjoy one of those parts or one-sixth of the pizza."

Kabens and Saya were overjoyed to have finally understood the concept of fractions.

Mommy cut the pizza into six slices.

"I can't wait anymore," Melaclap said, as she grabbed a slice and started to eat. Everyone else grabbed a slice and sat next to the fire. During lunch, they continued to talk about mathematics.

All of a sudden Janeed, who was sitting closest to the bookshelf heard a rumbling sound.

'The book of Jewels', which they had previously placed in the bookshelf had popped out. Everyone quickly turned their heads towards the book. They all knew that the next adventure was about to begin. Janeed grabbed the book, placed it in the middle and opened it.

A swirling bright light came out of the book brightening the room. As the light subdued, the children found themselves in the middle of a large city. They were near a grand building with a beautiful dome.

In front of this building, they saw a man with a green turban. He was surrounded by several other people. It appeared that he was a teacher explaining something to his students. As the children got closer, they heard him talking about mathematics. Suddenly, the students around this person gathered their books and notes, and walked away.

The teacher looked at the children with a smile and said, "Greetings my dear children! Welcome to the city of Baghdad."

He continued, "You must be wondering who I am. Let's walk inside and I will tell you much about myself and about this magnificent place, which is filled with knowledge from all around the world."

On the way to the building, the children politely introduced themselves. As they entered the hall, its grandeur overtook them. They all looked around and admired the beautiful building. They were awe-inspired by it, as they had never seen anything like it before.

For this adventure, they were transported in the 3rd century A.H. (9th century A.D.) in the city of Baghdad.

As the children looked around, the man in the green turban said. "Welcome to the remarkable 'House of Wisdom' or 'Bayt al-Hikma' as it is called in Arabic. I am Muhammad bin Musa Al-Khwarizmi. I was born in the year 163 A.H (780 A.D.)"

He continued, "did you know that the word 'Algorithm' is my name 'Al-Khwarizmi' in Latin?"

The children looked at each other with amazement. They had learned in school that a procedure of solving a problem or a computation is called an 'algorithm', yet they had no idea that this word referenced Al-Khwarizmi.

Khwarizmi continued to tell the children about the House of Wisdom, the place where he worked. "This place is the epicenter of knowledge. It is here, where you can find the smartest men and women from around the world, from all fields and professions."

As they walked through the building, they saw many scholars and scientists. Some were sitting around in circles, while others standing and talking to each other discussing different topics. There were others giving lectures to a group of people, and some writing and experimenting.

There was also a large library containing books in different languages and on variety of subjects from all over the world. All of them were getting translated to Arabic.

Khwarizmi brought the children into a room where he worked. Pages filled with beautiful geometrical drawings, equations, and calculations were spread around the room.

Kabens kindly asked, "Sir, could you please tell us more about your work?"

Khwarizmi said, "I am known for my amazing works in the field of Astronomy and Mathematics. Airplanes, computers, TVs, cars, video games, in fact all the modern electronics that you are familiar with will not be possible in the future without the work that I have done in this 'House of Wisdom'."

كتاب الخوارزمي

"My most significant contribution is the book that I titled 'Al-Kitāb al-Mukhtaṣar fī Ḥisāb al-Jabr wal-Muqābalah', translated in English as 'The Compendious Book on Calculation by Completion and Balancing'. From the name of this book, the field of 'Algebra' was started, and because of this, the world refers to me as the grandfather of mathematics and father of Algebra."

"So it was you who made this difficult subject that I was having such a hard time understanding," remarked Saya suddenly. That cheered everyone up.

Children sat on a round carpet as Khwarizmi continued to tell them about himself. There were some pictures and charts on the wall which he pointed towards as he explained different concepts to the children.

"It is through my work that the Arabic numerals will be popularized, which will eventually get used all over the world."

"In one of my books I explained how to calculate the volume of solids, the decimal system, and solutions of several different equations. My findings have been used in many practical fields to solve real life problems."

Janeed giggled whispering "like dividing up the pizza."

Al-Khwarizmi smiled and replied, "Exactly! without understanding and utilizing these concepts it becomes difficult to be fair in giving other's their equitable share.

Remember children, honesty and fairness in our dealings is very important for our societies to prosper."

Khwarizmi then took the children outside near a sundial. He explained how a sundial is used to tell the time during the day.

"I also wrote a book on sundials and how to best use them to calculate time during the day," he said.

"Wow!", exclaimed Ezzah, "that must have been really important and helpful for so many people. I can't imagine doing anything without knowing time."

"Absolutely," replied Khwarizmi, "especially for the Muslims, time is extremely important! So we can perform the five daily prayers on time."

"In my writings, I always drew diagrams that helped in explaining the idea better."

As everyone walked back inside Khwarizmi continued to tell them about his contributions.

"Children, have you ever wondered how big the earth is?"

"Yes", replied all in unison.

"I wondered as well!", Khwarizmi continued, "I worked very hard to figure out how to measure the distance around the Earth with much accuracy. I also helped in the construction of a world map. In another book that I wrote, titled 'Al Kitāb ṣūrat Al-Arḍ' ('The Image of the Earth'), also known as the 'Geography' I presented the coordinates of all the localities in the world. It is considered as a masterpiece work in the field of geography.

There was so much more to learn about Khwarizmi and his contributions to the various fields of science. However, the time was approaching for the children to return.

As Al-Khwarizmi bade farewell, he gave an advice; "Children, I hope that you continue to increase your knowledge and work hard every day to advance science to new heights."

The room was suddenly lit with a bright light. As the light diminished, children were back at Ezzah's house.

"That was a remarkable experience", said Heba, while everyone else nodded in agreement.

The snow had stopped falling and the children were now eager to go outside for sledding. As they walked outside, they continued to discuss what they had experienced, and decided to learn more about Al-Khwarizmi by asking their parents and teachers about him.

Al-Khwarizmi

The Great Mathematician

ACTIVITIES

Knowledge Review

1: Al-Khwarzmi's name in Latin is ___________.

A. Algebra B. Alexander C. Algorithm D. Aluminium

2: Al-Khwarizmi was born in the year __________A.H.

A. 249 B. 163 C. 136 D. 194

3: Al-Khwarizmi is known as the father of ________

A. Astronomy B. Mathematics C. Geometry D. Algebra

4: _______ is the place where Al-Khwarzmi worked.

A. Laboratory B. House of Pizza C. House of Wisdom D. Observatory

5: The 'Image of the Earth' was a book written by___________.

A. Al-Khwarizmi B. Ibn-Battuta C. Al-Razi D. Mariam Astrolabia

Answers: 1C, 2B, 3D, 4C, 5A

Al-Khwarizmi

The Great Mathematician

ACTIVITIES

Knowledge Review

1: Al-Khwarzmi's name in Latin is ___________.

A. Algebra B. Alexander C. Algorithm D. Aluminium

2: Al-Khwarizmi was born in the year __________A.H.

A. 249 B. 163 C. 136 D. 194

3: Al-Khwarizmi is known as the father of ________

A. Astronomy B. Mathematics C. Geometry D. Algebra

4: _______ is the place where Al-Khwarzmi worked.

A. Laboratory B. House of Pizza C. House of Wisdom D. Observatory

5: The 'Image of the Earth' was a book written by___________.

A. Al-Khwarizmi B. Ibn-Battuta C. Al-Razi D. Mariam Astrolabia

Answers: 1C, 2B, 3D, 4C, 5A

SUDOKU PUZZLE

2					4	8		
	6	7		2		9		
4			6		3		2	
				8				
					9			5
	9	8	5	6		1		7
								9
7		4						6

HELP AL-KHWARIZMI TO FIND HIS BOOK

About the Pioneer Series:

Nurturing courage, confidence and love of knowledge in young minds through stories on great individuals and leaders that transformed the world through their wisdom, inventions, discoveries and exploration.

Like, Share, Follow us on:

Instagram

www.instagram.com/pioneerbookseries

Facebook

www.facebook.com/pioneerbookseries

Youtube Channel

Pioneer Book Series for Kids

About the Author and Contributors:

Rafia Rehman, a mother of two has a Masters degree in Clinical Mental Health Counseling. She has worked at various agencies in United States of America and Pakistan providing mental health services to a diverse group of individuals including children. She is passionate about the concept of holistic education.

Dr. Abdul Rehman is a renowned Architect and a life long educator. He received his Ph.D in Architecture from the Ion Minco Institute of Architecture in Bucharest, Romania. He served as a professor and the Director of School of Architecture at the University of Engineering and Technology in Lahore, Pakistan. He has been a fellow at Dumbarton Oaks, Harvard University, and Massachusetts Institute of Technology, and has authored numerous books and publications. (www.drabdulrehman.com)

Umair Zia holds degrees in Electrical, and Systems Engineering and a graduate certificate in Mechanical Engineering. Serving a career in the Electric Power industry he held numerous technical and leadership positions. He has also served on the boards of non-profits, and as a teacher and Vice President of curriculum development at Al-Itqaan school in Worcester, MA.

About the Illustrator:

Muhammad Yousaf Rana is a career artist, caricaturist and illustrator. He has taught the art of caricature and illustration as well as conducted workshops at several institutions including the Oriental College of Arts and the University of The Punjab. He has a vast experience of illustrating children's books.

Integrity-Humbleness-Compassion

www.ingramcontent.com/pod-product-compliance
Ingram Content Group UK Ltd.
Pitfield, Milton Keynes, MK11 3LW, UK
UKHW060117300726
14090UKWH00002B/236

* 9 7 9 8 4 8 2 0 6 0 9 8 8 *